ABANDONED
But Not
FORGOTTEN

ABANDONED *But Not* FORGOTTEN

"ONE WOMAN'S TRUE STORY OF BEING ABDUCTED AS A CHILD. TO SCOURING THE PLANET FOR HER BIRTH PARENTS."

DANA PRIYANKA HAMMOND

XULON PRESS ELITE

Xulon Press
2301 Lucien Way #415
Maitland, FL 32751
407.339.4217
www.xulonpress.com

For more information or to book an event, contact Dana Priyanka Hammond at http://www.humantraffickinginc. com or visit http://www.danapriyankahammond.com

Printed in the United States of America

Paperback ISBN-13: 979-8-3304-9696-9
Ebook ISBN-13: 979-8-3304-9699-0

———

A Brand-New Slate
A pure white and clean canvas.
Every stroke tells a story; every stroke creates a detail.

———

FOREWORD

Specialty ice cream products, agricultural equipment for cows, rappers, multi-million-dollar homes, a boat restoration company in Belize, and shopping malls in Mozambique; these are just a few of the *thousands* of products, services, and people I've had to create marketing for since 1992.

If you had told me that I'd be helping a victim of human trafficking in India create a platform she can use to search for her birth parents, I would (sort of) believe that— and, at the same time, I wouldn't.

But, of course, meeting Dana just wasn't your typical referral. We're both authors in a book that has recently won a *Guinness Book of World Records* award (for the most authors signing a book simultaneously).

After being introduced to Dana, it quickly became apparent to me that this was a woman on a mission. Her story is shocking. If you don't know about it, you'll wonder how you would react if you were placed in the same position.

She's trying to end the horrible world of human trafficking, a multi-billion-dollar industry, and all with a newborn girl to raise.

Her resilience is beyond words; and she is not to be underestimated.

Of course, there is no guarantee that she (and her team, of which I'm honored to be a member) will be successful. We are certainly doing everything in our power to achieve her goal.

But even if we fall short, nobody could ever say that it was from a lack of effort or determination.

By the end of her story, you'll be glad you met Dana. My hope is that you'll want to join the effort to finally stop the truly despicable practice of human trafficking.

I'm honored to have met her, and I'm also humbled to be a part of this incredible ride.

Tim Burt

ACKNOWLEDGMENT

I dedicate this book to my Lord and Savior, Jesus Christ, the one who died on the cross and bled for my soul. He is both my heavenly and earthly Father in the absence of my father and the one who sits high on the throne. Thank you, precious Holy Spirit, for leading me on the right path in life as you continue to guide me.

I thank and give reverence to the Father, Son, and Holy Spirit for being the Trinity and the best thing that ever happened in my life. This book is all in God's hands to be led at His will.

I also dedicate this book to myself. I am thankful for the ability to start and see this project to fruition. I know that all things are possible through God who strengthens me.

CONTENTS

INTRODUCTION

———

This is an acknowledgment of what I must do. I must go forth and share my testimony of where God has brought me from. I must go forth and encourage those who need to hear from God. If He did it for me, He will do it for you. God predestined my life and has ordered my steps since birth. Therefore, He has also predestined yours. What He predestined; He foresees. What He foresees, He also watches over. The footsteps of a righteous man are ordered by the Lord, and no one can pluck you out of His hands. What the devil meant for bad, God meant for my good, He had a destiny and a plan for me.

This book is about my life experiences. I am going to walk you through the moments of my life that I remember from my youth until now (abandonment, adoption, homelessness, foster care, and the salvation and glory of the Lord). I have been told to, "Stop acting like the victim," but I humbly tell my story to edify people and give them hope so they can find strength in Jesus.

You do not have to bow down in acceptance of your circumstances. You are more than a conqueror, and your experience is a footstool. You are not your past. Your past is a divine setup that builds character for your future. You don't have to accept death but can accept life, life in your spirit, life in your soul, and life in your future. Your latter shall be greater. Do not let the devil or those he uses rob you of your future. The enemy's job is to steal, kill, and destroy whomever he can, devour through his divisive tactics of verbal and physical assault in order to decrease your confidence and self-esteem. You are beautifully and wonderfully made. The Lord knows the thoughts that He has toward you, to prosper you and bring you to an expected end. You can do all things through Christ who strengthens you.

If it had not been for God's hands in my life, I would have been dead a long time ago. His grace and mercy saved me. I thank the Lord for that. Ever since I was a young girl, people have said, "You should write a book about your life." When God saved me, He used others to inform me of His plans for my life; Thy will, not my will, be done. In 2008, God began convincing me heavily to write this book to touch the lives of others through my story and how I made it.

When I first started writing this book in 2008, I could only write two sentences, and then I gave up completely. I could not deal with my past and the pain it brought me while I was writing. Now in 2016, God has brought me a mighty long way and He keeps blessing me. As I write this book, my life in remembrance reminds me of how God cleansed me and made me over, He gave me beauty from my ashes.

I have to admit that God sure knows what He is doing. In spite of the challenge, God made it easier to write my story. He has empowered me with personal development and leadership with peace and joy. I pray that the life of an abandoned girl will give you hope, no matter the circumstances, for a new outlook on life and serve the purpose that was intended. Enjoy! yours truly, Dana.

Chapter 1

ABANDONMENT

———

In the previous book that I co-authored, *Tear the Veil Volume 2*, I mentioned what it was like for me to be abducted from my family. I carried you through deep emotions and the journey of what it felt like to be kidnapped and trafficked to an unknown place; I gave descriptive details of what it was like to go from one country to another in a foreign land, experiencing abuse from my first adoption in America after being placed in an orphanage. I would like to finally take the opportunity and launch off from that chapter in *Tear the Veil,* to tell the rest of my story, as well as revisit some things for those of you who haven't read that book. Here, I will be able to elaborate in further detail, which I did not share previously.

In this chapter, I likened kidnapping to abandonment because that's what it felt like. The truth is, I really was not abandoned. My kidnapping experience still gives me mixed emotions. I was flooded with feelings of abandonment until I discovered the truth, which is that I had been kidnapped and trafficked into slavery for whatever reason, whether it was sex trafficking, organ trafficking, labor trafficking, and/

or adoption trafficking. My hunch is that I was trafficked for adoption. I won't really know until I go in search of my birth family to find out the truth—to find out the full story behind exactly what type of trafficking I endured and how I got kidnapped from my family. As you can see, there are many forms of trafficking. Once I go on the journey to find my birth family, I will get to the bottom of it—where I can walk down the healing journey to be whole. My story begins when I found myself lost in a rice sack, prior to the day I was found on April 23, 1988.

In the never-ending movement of India, where people travel on dirty, unpaved roads, the cities are full of life and always active. There are crowds of people going around with rickshaws, mopeds, and bikes. Billboards are everywhere, big and small, advertising films that are two to three hours long, each with meaningful stories that grip audiences and change the lives and views of people who watch them. People gather together for festivals and holidays that spark the clouds with fireworks and colors in the times of every important event.

When I was only four years old, I remember being carried on someone's back in a rice sack. I believe it was a man carrying me, because I could hear the sound of his footsteps. By the sound, I could identify this man's strength. I realize now that, even then, I had the sensitivity to discern. I felt myself hanging like a sack of potatoes, but I was too afraid to move, slung over on his back, not knowing what's happening to me. I could hear this person's footsteps on a gravel road, walking, and understood the strength of the footsteps as he stepped down one foot at a time. As he lifted his legs, I was certain that I was being carried by a man walking in sandals. *Where is he taking me?* I thought. *Who is he?* I did not know. I didn't want to move or give him any indication that I was awake. If only I could figure out what was happening to me. But the biggest question was, *where am I going?* I sure would have loved to know. Where was my family? Was this a family member? NO! I knew something terrible was happening to me. I was balled up in a fetal position, wanting to stretch and move. The rice sack was cramped and uncomfortable. Lying in the same position for an extended period, I got a crick in my neck and my joints were tired of holding still.

I felt scared, so I just fell asleep again. I was tired, thirsty, hungry, hot, and itchy after being stuffed in that bag. I needed to reposition myself, but I could not. Not knowing what was going on, I didn't feel I should move or make a noise, due to my fear of the unknown. I was thirsty, wanting some water, as my mouth felt dry as a desert; cotton mouth was setting in. The itchy material of the bag poking me felt like little pins all over my body. I wanted to scratch myself. I was so hungry I could hear my stomach growl with the stomach juices churning inside. Tired still, my eyes were blurry and hazy, with film over them; I could not see clearly. I couldn't figure out why I was so tired. It was early morning; what was causing me to feel so sleepy? It was not a natural sleep, but one beyond regular rest. I can't recall what happened to me before I found myself lost in this rice sack, wondering how I ended up there. I see myself going somewhere in the hands of this unknown bad man. What was causing this terrible fear to come over me? I sensed something terrible was taking place, as though the hands of my destiny were ending too quickly for one so young. I would soon find out.

The funny part is I cannot recall anything before this. I cannot remember my parents' faces; I cannot recall my home; I cannot recall what I could have been doing. I don't even know exactly where I'm from, what city or state, but I know I am not from the part of India that this terrible man took me to. I couldn't possibly be! Too afraid to move, with this gnawing sleep that didn't feel normal, I felt that my hairline was sticky with sweat. I felt the significant wetness on my back, with my frock sticking to me from sweat. *It's hot in the bag*, I thought, *I need fresh air to breathe*, but my energy had dropped with my sleeplessness still drooping over me.

I look back to the year 1988, and I'm only four years old then. It's the year I see myself carried in a sack. I picture myself opening my eyes inside this brown, woven, hemp bag. I recognize this bag as an industrial-size rice sack that Indians use when they want to bag up large quantities of rice. I see myself hidden in this big bag, where I could not see anything outside but the beams of light coming through the tight, woven holes, indicating that it is morning time. The silhouettes of trees and their shadows passing over me, along with the brightly beaming sun, made me use my senses for awareness to recognize my surroundings. I could hear the morning birds chirping, cooing, and cawing. I had no other choice but to stop fighting my tiredness and allow myself to fall back to sleep.

Huddling together, holding myself, my own body heat was the only thing that kept me warm when the temperatures dropped during the evenings. It became cold throughout the night until early morning. Once the sun peaked its head out, the temperature grew to over ninety degrees; it was scorching. I had to deal with the temperature adjustment, as sweat made it even colder at night. When the temperature started cooling, my body started shivering with the wetness left behind, and it was chilly. Even though this relentless sleep didn't want me to wake up for anything, my suffering of cold didn't last long once I dozed off to sleep. I trusted and hoped for the best: that I wouldn't wake up to a nightmare of life—that I would be safe for those very moments of me being asleep. It was during those moments in between, when I found myself waking up, that I recognized new details with my ears and nose; I felt another place of my surroundings. I was putting more etches into my mind that painted a picture of what was really happening to me.

I normally wore a frock, no sweater or shoes. A lot of us usually go barefooted in my country. I don't know what time of day it was when I was kidnapped from under my parents' noses, but I suspect it happened at night. I can't imagine the grief my parents might have felt when they realized their baby girl was missing.

For this tall man with a shirt, a pair of pants, and sandals to do his job as a thief so effectively—to grab me when their eyes weren't on me, put chloroform over my mouth to knock me unconscious, and stuff me into a rice bag—he must have been watching me for a while before he attempted to move.

When you are four years old, you have no way of comprehending how something this traumatic is. So many children have endured things that I can't imagine myself going through, and yet, this was my reality. Like many of the victims who have already been living the life of this scary world, it also seems like my destiny is taking place; like it's been signed by the stars of my future.

The awful places these thieves take little children like me are either for sex trafficking, where they go through the process of being locked up in fear, starved, threatened with death, and forced into a room of darkness with no one to turn to until the pimps and madams deemed to choose.

When it's time for the child to get started as another one of their objects to please their clients (usually when they begin puberty), they undergo the brutal process of being abused and dressed in cheap clothing to make them look grown as young women. They endure body shaming and humiliation; they are given back-alley surgical procedures without proper care or treatment. They have to endure being cut in their privates in preparation for sexual servitude, until they are brutally mutilated. This causes various health problems, including the potentially higher risk of infection due to the use of dirty glass, razors, or scalpels.

Still bleeding, and without enough time to heal, they are forced to service their first client, who takes away their virginity, innocence, and virtue. Then, time and time again, seeing one person after another, serving them with no break or rest to heal, they are shamed and devalued as cash cows. The pimps and madams put so much fear in the child that the child has no option or choice to escape; and if the girl ever did, then it meant death.

Their bodies are left on the ground, on the streets of the cruel world where nobody cares. Victims have a hard time making it in life from childhood to adulthood; that is, if they do survive, barely breathing and hardly living.

The other direction a child goes is when these evil men force them to beg for money, putting fear in the child's life and forcing them to become nothing. Some get tortured with abuse and pain, and some often get a limb intentionally broken, cut, or brutally severed, along with their eyes gouged to make them blind or acid thrown on their faces and bodies to make them weak or feeble to the general public.

These children become hungry and starve, getting very desperate for money. If they don't bring something back to their "owners," they're subjected to another night of anguish, pain, and torture, which could mean death.

The last thing they need is for ordinary people to treat them like disgusting pieces of trash. They don't need to be called the untouchables or addressed like they aren't even human beings. They didn't choose to be kidnapped. It's unfair and it's cruel. They also need to have a voice and a choice.

Last but not least, adoption trafficking is another potential path these children's live's may take; the orphanages are no saving angels themselves. Don't misunderstand—I'm not saying all orphanages are this way—but I am saying the majority of the orphanages are, or have less than stellar track records. They hire people off the streets to kidnap children from those same streets, or from under their families' noses, to bring them to the orpahanges.

There, they can adopt them out illegally by making it legal. To put it simply, they either lie and tell parents they are going to give their children better education and send them off to school, which they will bring them back to them, or they kidnap children off the streets.

The orphanages then create legal documents that say the child has been abandoned and lie on the documents to state that there has been no trace of the families. Then they set them to legally get adopted through the court systems, where they make $10,000 or more per child to adopt the children away to other countries, taking advantage of the adoptive parents, the kids, as well as the birth parents.

The birth parents who do agree to send their kids off for better education (which they could not afford) are made to sign a contract. The sad part is, most of these parents are illiterate, and don't realize that they just consented to have their child be adopted in another country. They're unknowingly saying that they no longer wanted their own child any longer.

These three things have been prime examples of why little kids get stolen, even though there are many more reasons. But I wanted to give you at least three reasons as to why children get kidnapped and taken. Society has been blind to what's been going on around them to stop it. Until the day someone finally decides to do something about it, there won't be enough helping hands to help these children. But one day, enough hands will volunteer to make movements which will change lives of the devastated, lost, and dying.

These kids are forced into a slavery system that has been nothing but dirty money. The love of money is the root of all evil. What are the children to do? They should be allowed to be kids, with loving adults to protect and provide for them. These kids deserve great childhoods.

BEFORE I MADE IT OUT ALIVE

As soon as I got kidnapped, the stranger started traveling by foot all night until he reached the train, far away from my home. I have no idea how many hours I spent in that rice sack.

I woke up on a train, still in the rice sack; it was tied above my head and I could not get out. I was starving, stomach growling to be fed. My mouth was still dry as a desert. My eyes were blurry and could not focus. Since I could not see through the bag, I was trying to listen to what was around me. Inside, it was quiet—not a sound, no motion or noise, just silence. This was the first time I experienced this fear of unknowing silence. I could not escape nor do anything.

I heard the train slow down with a *shhh* noise, the steam whistling and hissing with smoke coming out and the tracks slowing down to a complete halt from its squealing sound.

Outside of the train, I could hear the people hustling and bustling, going here and there, having goods and items and things, talking in their language as if they had something important to say and somewhere important to go; bumping against one another; rushing and hasting to get on the train. It was like a crowd jamming in the entranceway, unable to get in until the train engineer finally releases the doors to open.

With the anxiousness of getting their first seats, they land their hands on the seats before the place starts filling up with a crowd; masses of people huddle in, having no room to move. Hearing the ruckus of a busy train station, I was glad to be at peace, where nobody was even bothering me.

Touching and feeling my way around, I could feel the seat where I was, feeling the energy of the train slowing down with no noise or sound in the subway. I don't know how long I was on the train, scratching my hands around the opening of the bag to see if I could escape. I felt safe to do so, but could not because the knot above my head was so tightly tied. I was cooped up, and I wanted out. Looking above, I felt like a prisoner deflated in frustration.

I tried to get out and look at my surroundings, to see where I was. I sensed that I was no longer with the wicked man; his presence was no longer around, and felt a lot more at ease. I was able to relax a little more, moving my muscles a bit to relieve tension. I was able to have the freedom to do so, without my life feeling like it was in danger. Being trapped inside, I just gave up and fell back to sleep.

I don't know how I came out of the train or who brought me out. However, eventually an Indian train station cop found me at Pune Railway Number 1, a train station in Pune, India.

Something must have taken place where things got mixed up with the thief who stole me. I never made it to the destination that he had chosen for me. Fortunately for me, whatever this thief planned, it didn't work out.

This is extremely rare. I must have been special to have escaped death. This was my last destination in Pune, India. This was at a time when Pune was prominent in sex trafficking (now, Mumbai holds that dubious honor).

Usually, cops in India work together with pimps and madams of prostitution to help put the kids in prostitution systems. The police in India are generally known to be just as dirty. It surprised me that an honest cop found me and brought me to a juvenile orphanage until the juvenile court could figure out what they wanted to do with me.

Escaping death has never felt sweeter.

Chapter 2
THE HOLDING PLACE

M y life has always been a mystery. I do not know my family, real birthday, nor the logic surrounding my abandonment. I was with them until I was four years old, but I honestly do not remember their faces. I simply have documents showing the day I was abandoned and found at Pune train station #1.

I later woke up in another strange place and did not know how I got there. I was surrounded by a bunch of children who I did not recognize. In this strange place, there were children ranging from young ages to around eleven-years-old. The writings of my Indian papers are so precious to me, and I cherish them because they are my only link to what happened to me. These writings describe that a police officer found me and took me to the orphanage. This was Mahila Seva Gram, the holding place.

It was a temporary facility for lost or abandoned children. I was there for three months until they found a permanent facility for me. My life would take a series of turns as I went through many processes from orphanage to adoption.

Because I was literally an "unknown" person, the official documentation at the holding place could only classify me as a baby girl with no known parents. No name, no family contact, or date of birth.

THE PROCESS

When social welfare conducts a search for birth parents, the social system places an advertisement in the media (e.g. TV, newspapers, etc.) of the surrounding areas where said minor was found with geographical data and a photograph. The release is advertised for an extended period of time (two to three weeks) to see if any birth relatives will come forward.

Memories of the orphanage are etched into my mind. The house mothers did not seem friendly at all. They were firm and very strict. They did what they had to do; I suppose. Discipline took the form of hard hits to the hand with long wooden sticks. Upon my arrival at the orphanage, my caretakers (called house mothers) took me through an intake process. I vividly recall being lined up with other children, and our heads were shaved bald to prevent the communal spread of lice. There was no distinction given from one child to the other. To our caregivers, we were all the same.

Next, we were immunized and then made to stand in another line to take a bath, all of us, boys, and girls, in the same dirty water. In retrospect, this reminded me of the old movies I had watched about Soviet Union camps during the war.

In the orphanage, school was private. Boys and girls attended this school, and uniforms were mandatory for all. I remember we all gathered to recite the Pledge of Allegiance for both the American flag and the Indian flag. Afterwards, we were dismissed and dispersed to our various classes. We learned the alphabet and the order of numbers, which was very difficult for me. I was confused about the who, what, where, when, and how of learning. I was placed in school with the expectation to learn without an assessment benchmark.

During lunch time, it would be so hot from the torturous sun that we preferred to sit on the porch in the shade. We never ate while at school. After school, we would return to the orphanage where meals were prepared for us. This would also be our playtime. When we became thirsty, we were sent out to the middle of the field to the water well. This was the only time we were permitted to go and drink. We drank from a water spout.

I met a girl who became my best friend. She was one of the first to grab me by the hand and introduce me to the other kids. She was older and she paraded me around as if I were her little baby doll. I remember how I would follow her everywhere, even down to the apartment complex by a tree. She would often visit that tree to call out to her mom who was on the upper level where they lived in order to get her attention. Her mom would often throw down food for us to eat. One day I was looking for her, and she was gone. I never saw her again after that and was heartbroken. She was the only friend I had and the only person who showed me love. To this day, I don't know what happened to her.

I remember them giving us new toys. The girls were given dolls and the boys were given other toys. After dinner and playtime, we were sent to bed. In bed, we lay side by side on the floor. Late one night, I had to go to the restroom. The restroom was down a dark hallway. Suddenly, a big, fat kitty cat appeared, walking around. He was a stray that lived around the building. The cat was huge, almost as big as me. I became so afraid, but I had to use the bathroom really badly, so I quietly tiptoed behind the cat, following him as he disappeared into the stalls. I looked up and there he was, blocking the stall. Frightened, I couldn't wait and had an accident. I left my wet pants behind and sped off, crying as I went back to bed. Little did I know that this would be my last day at this orphanage. Unbeknownst to me, they were preparing transfer papers for relocation to a long-term facility, where I would await adoption.

The next morning, a liaison from the Bharatiya Samaj Seva Kendra (BSSK) facility was sent to transport me from the holding place to a BSSK orphanage. On the way to the new orphanage, we had to stop at the courthouse and the doctor's office. Finally, I arrived at BSSK, transported on a scooter. The people there were much nicer. They gave me a new name, "Punam," which means, "full moon." At the end of the process, a certificate of abandonment was issued to legalize me for adoption. I spent the remainder of my time in India with BSSK. The document below is the certificate of abandonment, which is a legal documentation that the courthouse created. This process would be repeated again before adoption.

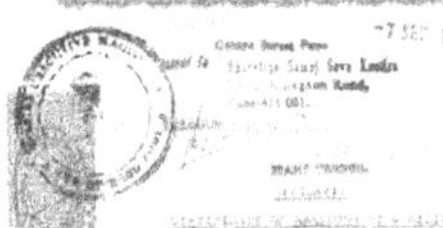

1. Child's Arrival Status (For the 1st Report only)

Punam was found abandoned dn railway platform, Pune. She was kept on remand in Mahila Seva Gram. After paper publication nobody came to claim her, she was short committed to BSSK for her better future, permanent rehabilitation.

III.

Social Background : These details are required to give adoptive parents details of the child's social history i e. brief background of the natural parents and circumstances necessitating the child's abandonment. Please **do not** give identifying information such as name and address of natural parents or relatives : Punam was found abandoned on 23/4/88 at Pune trainstation by railway police. She was about 4 yrs old. On the same day she was kept on remand in an institution in Pune for protection and acare. Efforts were made by the institution to trace her parents but in vain. She was then committed to BSSK / BSSK also made efforts to trace her parents but in vain. Worker also spoke to Punam but she could only recollect names and instances of

Aug.91

Chapter 3

PERMANENT REHABILITATION

Next stop, Bharatiya Samaj Seva Kendra (BSSK). On August 26, 1991, efforts were made again by BSSK to find my birth family, Pune. BSSK is a public charitable trust registered under the Bombay Public Trust Act of 1950. It provides welfare services to families and children in need and is licensed as a fit person's institute by the director of social welfare. It is also recognized by the ministry of social welfare of the government of India for the purpose of international adoption.

Interestingly enough, they issued the advertisement again, indicated by the words, "...the first time was." This seems to be a measure of safety to assure the birth parents could not be located. However, it is noteworthy to mention the following:

> "As per BSSK, even if information about my birth parents were left with me in the rice sack, the orphanage is unable to release this information, because of the safety of the parent."

In accordance with legal establishments in India, even after years past, if an adopted child had a desire to learn of their biological parents, it would have to be done so in their research. Most adoption agencies have this same practice, herein lies the difference between most countries and India. In India, even after many years, if it is discovered that a young woman had a child out of wedlock, they could potentially be harmed."

There were lots of kids in the orphanage, and some of whom were disabled. Some suffered disabilities as minor as a cleft lip or as major as conjoined legs. My health was poor due to nutritional deficits and physical infirmities (scabies, old heel rickets, malnutrition, upper respiratory condition, and a lisp). According to the World Health Organization, it was difficult to measure the health of a population in developing countries because of inconsistencies in vital statistic registration. India was among four developing countries that lacked sufficient data on its population due to the many problems that existed in the culture. Hence, it is not surprising that I was born with and suffered such nutritional deficits and physical infirmities. They had to do hypothetical guessing of my age based on physical examination through an X-ray of my bone structure and marrow. Aside from non-invasive procedures, much was based on if-then theoretical perspectives. This was a natural process to determine the age of an individual who did not have a birth record. If I was four years old on April 23rd 1988, then it seems the process to determine my age was spot on. My gut was correct. I was four. I am happy to know that births must be documented now. It is a tragedy to be abandoned with no knowledge of who you are, where you are from, and to have no sense of belonging.

Nevertheless, I have fond memories of India. I am of Hindustani descent. We had many cultural activities. I had the chance to experience celebrations of holidays and festivals. Art appreciation was influenced by creative arts, shows, creation of color throws, and much more. Now, Indian food, certain smells, and cultural activities help me to embrace my culture (e.g. dance rituals).

In retrospect, I remember being taught about the roles of family with our dolls. We each had dolls that we loved, and we would adopt certain family roles to act out the importance of marriage, family, and parenting. Our sleeping quarters had bunks, cots, and one television. We had to share everything. We enjoyed shows like *Tom and Jerry*, Charlie Chaplin, and old Hindi movies. Our attire consisted of pretty frocks (dresses) and sandals. We also had our ears pierced, which was traditional for the culture.

On another note, our days were filled with fun routines on the playground as well. Some days, I was frightened by cobras because of the construction that was going on to build the new facility. The cobras were forced out of their habitat because of the construction. Usually, they only come out when the temperature drops because the temperature during the day is normally over 100 degrees.

I remember seeing other kids get adopted. The adoption agency would give the adoptee photo albums, toys, and other things the family wanted him or her to have in preparation for adoption. Sometimes, the families would come and visit to see their new child. Their faces would beam with light about the expectations of adoption. I wanted to feel this excitement and be adopted as well.

Then, that miraculous day had arrived. It had been one year now at BSSK. BSSK was responsible for communicating with families that wished to adopt. The time had come, and there was a potential family for me. "Mr. X, an American National, has applied to appoint him as a guardian of minor Punam."

FINDINGS SUGGEST:

Mr. and Mrs. X had two male children and always wanted a daughter. The two initially adopted a baby girl from the BSSK, who died as a result of congenital heart disease. Both parents were employed at the time of petition. It was reported that the home was secure for me, and the family was approved by the International Children's Service, USA, to adopt me. Their finances were deemed sufficient with savings and investments for securing my future in a happy home. They were also considered physically and mentally capable of caring for a young child, and the social welfare had no objection to appointing the petitioner as guardian. Prior to finalizing the decision of adoption, additional steps were taken in search of biological parents. The petitioner was hereby appointed guardian and required to report every three months for two years on the welfare of the child and every six months for five years to social welfare and the Indian council of social welfare. I had gone from one institution to another, but this was my last stop before getting adopted. Every placement was different. The constant was that I was always in a state of not knowing. I never knew what to expect next.

Finally, I received my very own photo album from my potential family. I was so excited. I was curious about them and was excited about feeling the love my friends felt. BSSK began the necessary steps to get my passport and other legal documentation in order. Since there was no documentation to verify my birth, the orphanage produced a necessary affidavit to get my green card to America. I was given my gifts and legal and health documents, an affidavit, and other paperwork along with the letter to my adoptive parents.

Letter from the Orphanage to Adoptive Parents:

Dear adoptive parents,

The long wait has ultimately come to an end. Your special child is right before you to see, touch, hug, and kiss.–Punam

We are sure the wait hasn't been easy. It must have been filled with tension, anxiety, happiness, and days of just gasping at the photograph sent to you, wondering whether your child will be what you imagined her to be? And, is she?

Does she look like what you thought? Is the color the same as your imagination? Is the height just right or the weight seem a little less? Do her eyes sparkle as much as you imagined and is she making any effort to reach out to you?

This little child of yours, as small as she is, has a mind too. One which certainly has some kind of expectations, and months have gone into preparation of your little one in explaining the fundamentals of Mommy and Daddy. Today, bang, they're right in front of her eyes. This is her reality after leaving behind the security of a home, even if it is an institution, the familiar faces, her little cot on which she sleeps, the usual food she eats and few prized possessions, friends and favorite people she left to begin a new life with you.

We are sure that you have given a lot of thought to these aspects mentioned above, but it is our hope that through this brief letter, you may be able to understand your child still better. Having opted to adopt an older child, we are sure you realize the importance of having a lot of patience and understanding toward the child.

A child in an institution does not have his or her own room, cot, toys, or clothes. Everything belongs to everyone and things are just shared. Coming into her new home, she is going to be happy to have things of her own. But this is going to take time, in spite of having her own room. She might not want to sleep alone, as that is something she is not used to. At first, she is going to get overwhelmed by all the comforts and luxuries that are new. It is likely that she will try to fiddle with the knobs of the TV, VCR, or music system.

Your child has probably not had an opportunity to be treated as a baby. Punam might demand your attention and regress in age. We do try to initiate discipline amongst our children, but often, there might not be consistency in this due to different staff twenty-four hours of the day. The dos and don'ts will be left up to you to initiate.

"Will our mom and dad shout and spank us?" is the question often asked with wide and sometimes frightened eyes. "When a person loves you, he also has a right to shout or spank you when you do something wrong," is what we normally tell our children. Have you ever given thought to how much your child has gone through in this short span of life?

Changing institutions, sometimes seeing new faces, and having to adjust to all kinds of new things like the surrounding staff who handle the children, food, and companions are their reality. Sometimes, little ones even ask us, "After we see our mommy and daddy, do we come back?" It is going to take her time to realize that this time, her change of scene is final. On account of these changes, it is natural that the child is going to have a feeling of insecurity until she gains her confidence in you. Insecurity may lead to inhibitions, thereby not allowing her to express her likes and dislikes. This may also be the result of some earlier traumatic situation that she might have faced.

On the other hand, the insecurity may cause your child to eat a lot and maybe more than she should. We try to give our children in the institution as much a variety of food as we can. Yet they never have the opportunity to watch adults eat and see the other foods that may be available. They will see a variety of different foods at your place, and she might get carried away. So, the right limits will have to be set by you before you have a tummy problem on your hands.

At BSSK, we do have a dog, but the concept of him being a pet is not really what is in the children's mind. If you do have a pet, give your little one some time to get acquainted with the animal and gradually let them become friends. Our children have not attended a formal school; they attended a private class on the campus of BSSK. Hence, having to go to a school outside of home and alone during schooling hours will be a totally new experience for them.

How many times have you asked yourself how you're going to communicate when your child arrives?

- Will she understand what you speak?
- How will you know when she wants something?
- How will you reassure her? Language is going to be a barrier for a short while. But will she learn to speak the way you do? The only language she will understand is love.
- Our children get a little aggressive sometimes playing with each other. They may tend to swap toys, pinch, or tease each other. We know the path leading to parenting a child, particularly an older adopted child, is going to have its share of ups and downs.
- We can tell you that your child is as anxious as you are. If you ever face any discomfort or difficulty in

bringing up your child, please do not hesitate to write to us, contact international child services, or seek any professional help. Someday in life, we hope you will be able to visit BSSK with your child, who will not remain a little one. With our warmest and sincere wishes for a happy future.

It is noteworthy to mention that this letter outlined critical points of clarity for the adoptive parents to consider in my care. Important factors were health and well-being, adaptation to the environment, coping with language barriers, and the implementation of processes to provide me with the love and care that any child deserves.

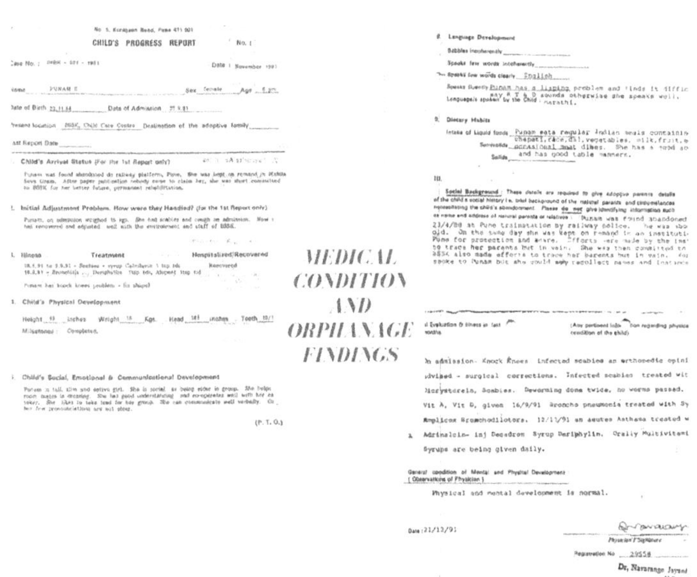

No. 5, Ferguson Road, Pune 411 001

CHILD'S PROGRESS REPORT   No. 1

Case No. : BSSK - 521 - 1981   Date : November 1991

Name   PUNAM E   Sex Female   Age   6 yrs.

Date of Birth 23.11.84   Date of Admission 27.9.91

Present location   BSSK, Child Care Centre   Destination of the adoptive family _______

Last Report Date _______

Child's Arrival Status (For the 1st Report only)

Punam was found abandoned on railway platform, Pune. She was kept on remand in Mahila Seva Gram. After paper publication nobody came to claim her, she was short committed to BSSK for her better future, permanent rehabilitation.

Initial Adjustment Problem. How were they Handled? (for the 1st Report only)

Punam, on admission weighed 15 kgs. She had scabies and cough on admission. Now she has recovered and adjusted well with the environment and staff of BSSK.

Illness	Treatment	Hospitalized/Recovered
18.1.91 to 2.9.91	Scabies + syrup Calmibron 1 tsp tds	Recovered
16.2.91	Bronchitis - Doriphylin Tsp tds, Alupent 1tsp tid	

Punam has knock knees problem - (in shape)

Child's Physical Development

Height 33 inches   Weight 15 Kgs.   Head 18½ inches   Teeth 18/1
Milestones : Completed.

Child's Social, Emotional & Communicational Development

Punam is tall, slim and active girl. She is social, as being eldest in group. She helps room mates in dressing. She has good understanding and co-operates well with her care takers. She likes to take lead for her group. She can communicate well verbally. Only her few pronounciations are not clear.

(P. T. O.)

8. Language Development

Babbles incoherently _______

Speaks few words incoherently _______

Speaks few words clearly   English

Speaks fluently   Punam has a lisping problem and finds it difficult any R T & D sounds otherwise she speaks well.
Language/s spoken by the Child : Marathi.

9. Dietary Habits

Intake of Liquid foods   Punam eats regular Indian meals containing chapati, rice, dal, vegetables, milk, fruit, & occasional meat dishes. She has a good appetite and has good table manners.
Semisolids
Solids

10.

Social Background : These details are required to give adoptive parents details of the child's social history i.e. brief background of the natural parents and circumstances necessitating the child's abandonment. Please do not give identifying information such as name and address of natural parents or relatives : Punam was found abandoned 23/4/88 at Pune trainstation by railway police. She was also old. On the same day she was kept on remand in an institution Pune for protection and care. Efforts were made by the inst. to trace her parents but in vain. She was then committed to BSSK also made efforts to trace her parents but in vain. We spoke to Punam but she could only recollect names and instances

Evaluation & illness in last 6 months   (Any pertinent information regarding physical condition of the child)

On admission- Knock knees Infected scabies an orthopedic opinion advised - surgical corrections. Infected scabies treated with Merystareln, Scabies. Deworming done twice, no worms passed. Vit A, Vit D, given 16/9/91 Broncho pneumonia treated with Sy Amplicox Bronchodilotors. 12/11/91 an acutes Asthama treated with Adrinalcin- inj Decadron Syrup Dariphylin. Orally Multivitami Syrups are being given daily.

General condition of Mental and Physical Development
(Observations of Physician)

Physical and mental development is normal.

Date : 21/12/91

Physician's Signature

Registration No   29558

Dr. Navarange Jayant
M.D, D.C

This has been read, understood and accepted by us.

PUNAM'S MEDICAL REPORT

Punam aged 7 yrs was brought to us on 27th August 1991 and has found to have severe knock knees and scabies with secondary infection. She has definite gait abnormalities and as per the opinion of the orthopaedic surgeons in Sassoon and Inlaks hospital. She requires corrective surgery.

The cause of this abnormality could be either old healed rickets or as a birth defect. She is getting intermittent bronchospasm also.

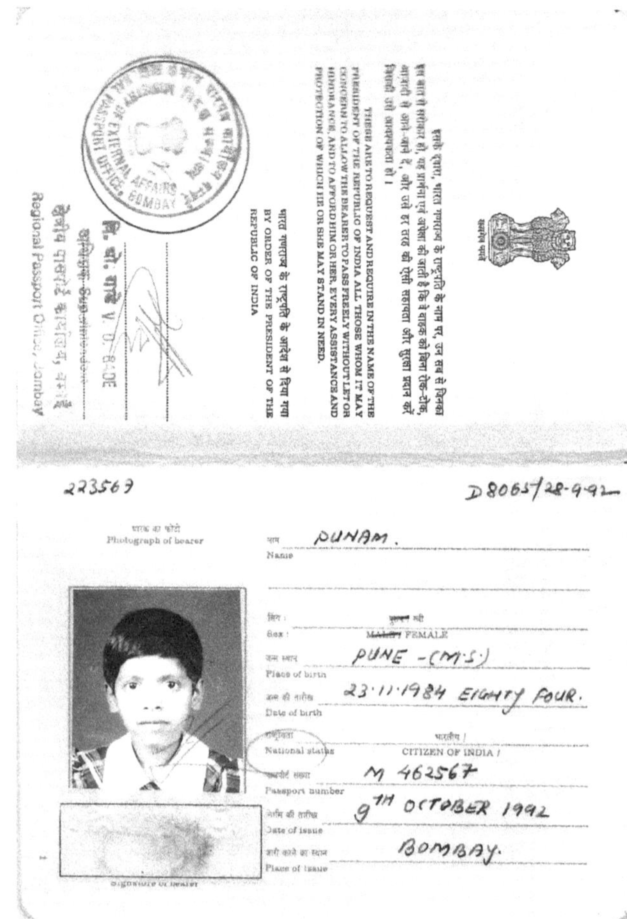

Permanent Rehabilitation

Medical Evaluation & illness in last three months.

(Any pertinent information regarding physical condition of the child)

1. On admission- Knock Knees infected scabies an orthopedic opinion advised - surgical corrections. Infected scabies treated with inj. Dicrystcrein, Scabies. Deworming done twice, no worms passed. Orally

2. Vit A, Vit D, given 16/9/91 Broncho pneumonia treated with Syrup Amplicox Bronchodilotors. 12/12/91 an aeutes Asthama treated with inj.

3. Adrinalcin- inj Decadron Syrup Deriphylin. Orally Multivitamins and Iron Syrups are being given daily.

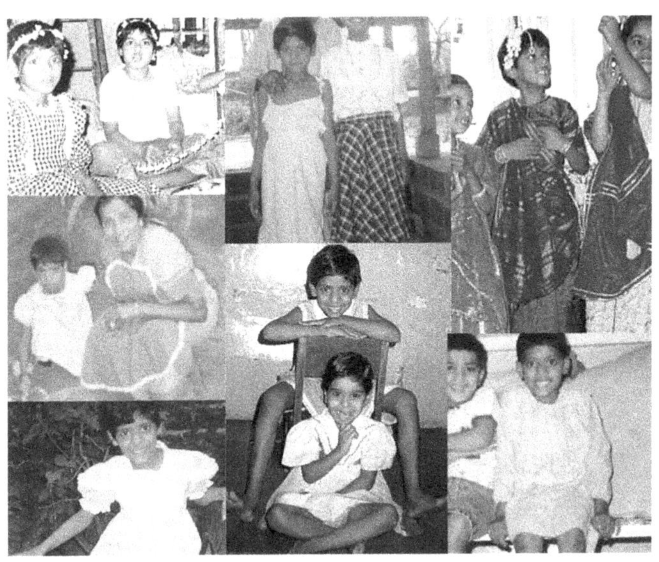

29

Chapter 4

BEHIND CLOSED DOORS

I t is 1992. Another adoptee and I are woken up by one of my house moms very early in the morning, while everyone is fast asleep, probably about 3:00 a.m. There are usually several rotating house moms who look after the various-sized children: from small, newborn infants to eight-year olds.

I have been sleeping on the top bunk of the bed that I am sharing with another child. Too sleepy to wake up, my little body feels groggy. It isn't normal for me to wake up at this hour. I'm able to climb down the ladder, stumbling all over, not knowing what I'm supposed to be doing. It is unusually different, and this is beyond new.

Why was I awakened? For what? I didn't understand why they woke us so early. Looking back, it all makes sense. I remember children being there one day and gone the next. After hours kept down the confusion for the children on both sides—those who leave behind the only family they have known, and those children who may question why they have not been selected for adoption.

I didn't know it was the day for me to leave India for good. This was the day that would be a huge milestone to the next level. I recognized the house mom getting another girl ready, helping her to get dressed, which indicated to me what I was supposed to be doing.

We prepared for our permanent departure of the orphanage. My house mom packed our unique, bright-colored silk lehenga dresses; the orphanage made for us for special occasions, so we could wear them one day to mark our traditions with brand-new metal bangles that fit our tiny wrists perfectly. She also packed our new floral-colored Indian sandals, along with our travel toothpaste and toothbrushes, photo albums of our new adopted families, doctor's x-rays, Indian documents, passports, and a sweater to keep us warm in our travels. Our bags were set to go.

We took our time to brush our teeth and hair and throw on our clothes. As soon as we finished, we were whisked away for the night. We rushed out the doors so we could make it to wherever we were going. I wanted to take my favorite dolly that I loved playing with so much, but instead I decided to leave it behind for the next child to enjoy.

In the orphanage, I took her everywhere. I did not want anyone else to have her while I was there. But now, I wanted another child to feel the love that I had.

As we were leaving, our house mother grabbed hold of our hands, one on each side, and brought us outside of the orphanage through the outside doors. Emerging from the doors, we came down the stairs, and I felt the cold air hit my face as we were led to our three-wheeled rickshaw. Our driver seemed anxious to take us, and hastened us along.

We had our frocks, sandals, and sweaters on, feeling the brisk cool of the night. Our house mother guided us up to the seat in the back of the rickshaw. She sat in the middle, and we sat on either side of her. We were off to the airport. Destination: America. As the rickshaw moved swiftly, the brisk wind blew against our faces. I could feel my nose and ears going from the cold air on my face. I was glad to have my neck and head somewhat covered with my silk scarf to protect me a little.

With a fast-going rickshaw, we got to the airport. It's a building I had never seen before, and I soon discovered new things along this journey, as we made the deadline.

Our house mother checked us in and got our boarding passes. We carried our little bags on our sides. We hardly had much with us, making traveling easy with nothing but our small valuable goods and the clothes on our backs.

She rushed us through security, bringing us to our exit. Everything is brand new and looks massive in a child's eyes.

As my wondering eyes got big, I looked around curiously, but we didn't take any time to stop and see anything. It all made my head spin; it was a lot to see, so busy with all the commotion. So far, everything had been rushed, as if she had been instructed to be on a mission, getting her job done as she was commanded.

We flew from Pune to Mumbai. We were the first ones to be seated, having special accommodations because we were little children; we settled in before the plane got filled with people. As minor children, our house mother was with us all the way through the trip.

Our long flight finally landed in New York, and I said bye to the friendly flight attendants who made me smile so much. The airport was immense compared to what I had just seen in India.

We were favored by the Delta flight attendants, who kept their eyes on us while we were in mid-air on our way to our new country, America. They gave us a doodle pad, coloring crayons, and papers. The stewardess presented us with Delta Airline pins as a departure gift to remember them by. I enjoyed the lovely flight attendants always checking on us.

It did not hit me until that day that I was leaving my own country. I felt sad, recognizing that I might never see my homeland again, seeing people who looked entirely different from me. It was a lot to absorb as a little eight-year-old kid, especially not knowing any English.

As soon as we arrived at New York Airport, I saw that it was even bigger, with even more crowds from different countries. We had to pick up our feet, running, while our house mom walked swiftly to get to our connection.

The next flight was on a smaller plane, this time to go to Chicago O'Hare Airport. It seemed to take about another couple of hours before arriving. I started getting used to this, flying from airports to airport. Upon landing, it was time to say goodbye to our house mom, who had taken us on this long journey to finally arrive at our destination.

On November 6, 1992, I safely arrived in America—finally—for adoption.

Our house mom stood there at the arrival area at the airport. I did not know why she was just standing there. All I know is that she was the last familiar face that I was comfortable with at the time. I didn't want to let go of her hand, so I stood by her side for comfort.

As soon as she let go of our hands, I heard screeching, screaming, joy, and laughter. I saw the girl who came with me get very excited and happy, jumping up and down in celebration and running right into the open arms of her new family, who approached her. With acceptance, love, and delight, she was instantly attached to them. I felt my heart melt for her, and desired the same thing that she was experiencing. You immediately felt the love in the airport for her.

Standing there like a bump on a log, not knowing what to do, I waited, not seeing anybody approach me. Turning my head back, I saw my house mom leave and seek security to no avail. With no hesitation, she walked out of my sight to go back home. She must have recognized both adoptive families before stepping off.

Finding it hard to swallow, I felt separation anxiety! I couldn't help but feel scared and insecure. My house mom went back to the only home I knew. My concern rose as my house mom left without looking back. I didn't want her to leave! Who was there to receive me? I didn't recognize anyone. The airport was busy, full of people, and I didn't want to be left alone. She just left me there standing by myself. Feeling my feet glued to the floor, I couldn't move. I didn't *want* to move.

Reality hit me; my life was changing at that very moment, left with total strangers with whom I had no connection or bond, never developing any association with the family the orphanage picked for me. Since the correspondence was weak, I didn't know whom to look for in this new place. Some of the kids at the orphanage developed bonds with their new families through phone calls, visits, and love letters. Moreover, the kids formed lasting memories of their new families, who were familiar with their faces, voices, and, most importantly, intentions. Having never received any of those connections, and not recognizing who was there to pick me up, I waited with heartfelt anticipation.

Recognizing that my house mom wasn't coming back, I was left alone for the first time, faced with an uncertain future. My country—my culture, the environment, the food, smells, colors, and the way of life—were gone from me.

In that very moment, with my heart beating fast and my hands sweaty, I felt jittery. My only security blanket was removed from me. I wanted my family back; I wanted my country back. *Help!* I thought. *I don't want to say goodbye! My whole life is torn apart. India just deserted me!*

Finally, I noticed an older white couple appear before me, standing there with blank looks on their faces; they were looking at me across the way. I wondered if these were the people I was supposed to go with. Them standing there made it feel like an eternity; they just stared at me. There was none of the excitement I'd expected upon seeing me— there was no interaction, reaction, move, sound, or emotion, along with no welcoming joy, hugs, or kisses. No celebration or gathering of the whole family. My arrival didn't get celebrated like I witnessed the other girl.

A bad feeling came over me, seeing them for the first time. Something in my spirit and soul didn't want to leave. They seemed scary; I didn't like their vibe. With frightened eyes and nowhere to turn, I felt like I was being forced to go with them.

This awkward greeting turned out to be even weirder. Truthfully, they didn't know what to do with me. A cold chill went down my spine as darkness fell before me. There was something dark about them. Feeling like the orphanage made a mistake, I thought these people couldn't possibly be it for me! These people couldn't be the ones that the orphanage matched me with! I felt like the orphanage just threw me to the wolves, without even carefully considering my life! What kind of jeopardy had they just put me in?

With no hello spoken during this time of approach, the woman took my familial sandals away from me, putting big clunkers on my feet. This is something I was not familiar with. Why did I have to put them on? I did not know then that they were called "boots," having never seen footwear like that before. They then put this puffy thing on me, zipping it up. I felt buried in this big thing. I did not know what it was or why I had been put into it. It was my first time putting on a snowsuit with a coat. It felt like I was being buried alive.

With no love or fire in their eyes, safety and security were issues with me. I didn't feel safe. Not knowing where I fit in, I couldn't get this uncomfortable feeling out of me;

I was not happy or settled in my heart. There'd been no bridge built between them and me, India to America.

Wasting no time leaving the airport, it just became business. I wanted the love that I witnessed other children receive from their new families, like the exciting reach-outs, the anticipation in the new family's hearts, their voices of excitement at getting their child; I wanted phone calls, storytelling, new toys, cards, and travel visitations to India to see their child. It had been inevitable that these people would be strangers to me. The other girl's new family started disappearing from us, while going on their own way. We went our own way to our separate realities.

In my new family's car, I got placed in the back seat with the seatbelt on. I felt a lot colder than what I was used to, not knowing it was called *winter*; I didn't even know what winter was! It was night, and the city seemed cleaner, brighter, and more up-to-date than any city I had ever seen or known. The air was crisper, not dusty, and the atmosphere was different than what I was accustomed to experiencing.

Driving away from the airport, I started seeing the airport get smaller this night, going to another unknown place. I saw white stuff on the ground that I had never seen before; I came to learn that it's called snow. I gazed out into this new land and wondered about this new place, looking around and seeing a bright city with lit roads. It was late, and my eyes had become heavy. It was a long journey on the way. I couldn't keep my eyes open anymore, so I fell asleep.

We arrived at a house in a small town called West Liberty in Iowa. I had never seen houses like this before; it was a stand-alone rambler, with three bedrooms with a big finished basement.

We arrived about five or six a.m.; my new parents took me in with them to this new, strange place I now called home. I was scared and alone, with no affection. The woman instantly undressed me and put cute, warm pajamas on me. This was a different kind of clothing, and I liked them.

Soon after this, she guided me to my new bed in a big room. I had never slept by myself before, and the silence was deafening. I desired more security, or at least to be tucked in. The lights got turned off, and I heard my new, unfamiliar parents going into their room to sleep; I immediately got up in this strange place, cold and afraid, wanting comfort. Everything was quiet and I didn't know what to think. I went into the hallway, wanting some human interaction, but no one was around. I stood there crying, wanting my need to be fulfilled and not wanting to be alone.

The elderly woman got up, came out of her room, and pushed me to go into my room. She walked me to my room once more, without tucking me in and without any affection. She stood there watching me get in my bed, and then left, shutting the door behind her. I was admonished to lie down into this new room, in the daybed. I put covers over my head, feeling scared. I had never felt this scared. Everything was brand new, and I was by myself for the first time, outside of my comfort zone.

I had officially been isolated for the first time, with no other children to play with or have any relatable connection with; I was separated into a corner of life where everything seemed lonely and big. No time for introductions to this new world, or even to understand the transition; I found myself forced to accept a different way of living where there was a vast cultural difference.

My adoptive mother took care of my daily needs temporarily. She bathed me, fed me bland food, and enrolled me in a school. That sums up most of her responsibilities to me, causing the beginning stage activities to be short-lived.

Neither of the parents did any parent-daughter activities, nor did either of them take the time to interact with me, which led me to question why they even adopted me in the first place. Any learning about the qualities of life, so far, had come from school and not from home.

Moreover, there was no structure, no foundation, no meaningful time invested in teaching me the do's and don'ts, the rights from the wrongs. I was left alone and neglected. It was a crucial part of my life to be protected and loved, entirely covered by an adult who would take his/her time to value me. I needed someone to spend time with me; someone to teach me things; someone to hold me and tell me that everything was going to be alright—that mistakes are mistakes, and I could try to do better.

I desired to be nurtured by someone. From my observation, my schoolmates received that quality time from their parents, and I wondered why I never did. It got lonely being by myself day in and day out, without the real meaning of family. It made me numb to the whole world, leaving me to fend for myself. I became numb from anger, bitterness, and isolation—what was I supposed to do?

I couldn't imagine leaving a child helpless to defend and fend for him- or herself in this world, because a child doesn't have the mental capacity to survive on his/her own. Just the thought of it leaves me terrified! Some people shouldn't be given the parental privileges of having children. My adoptive parents left me trying to figure things out on my own, having no clue what I was supposed to be doing.

Down the road, I discovered that my adoptive mother was a severely damaged human being. Growing up, she became the second mother to her younger siblings. She had many responsibilities on her shoulders, taking care of her siblings while her mother was derelict in her responsibilities. Her father became intoxicated almost daily, abusing her mom physically as often as he drank. Unfortunately, my adoptive mom became next in line to suffer generational abuse by her father, thus not having a quality childhood; she took on adult responsibilities and stress. She coped by doing what she experienced.

This pattern of behavior she exhibited was completely manipulative, intimidating, and abusive. Narcissistic in nature, she possessed and ruled over the home, controlling both the finances and her husband; she became an emotional volcano to the point that anything could set her off. If she didn't like something, she would badger until it wore you out. Everything always became dramatic. You couldn't be around her without feeling drained by her negativity.

My adoptive mother frequently demeaned, intimidated, bullied, and belittled me, even though I was a child who didn't know any better; a child who didn't understand what was taking place. I never received the real security or covering that I longed for. Her egoism and lack of empathy caused her to pay no attention to her natural, motherly instinct.

In a narcissistic personality, being the center of attention is paramount. It's worse when all the care is taken off the person and is demanded to put into a child, who requires the attention and love. Whatever my adoptive mom's shortcomings were, she felt entitled to oppressively punish for minor things.

Her insecurities make her suspicious of my motives and behaviors, and thus are her reasons for becoming angry with me frequently. I tested her nerves without really understanding how. Her bitterness became damaging, her anger became too much of a burden, and I became her reason for everything. She dumped everything on me like a garbage canwhile also making me her punching bag.

My adoptive father was, to put it kindly, impotent. He couldn't stop her because he was too weak and emasculated, lacking a voice in his own house. She ran the show, and he worshiped her. He would watch his wife say and do all manner of abusive things to me and wouldn't even utter a word or stand up to do anything.

I wonder if he was scared of her also. He often let her do anything she wanted with me, and it didn't even phase him. He didn't have anything to do with me, and we never had any connection.

He let his wife take care of all my needs, but, even then, I never got what I truly needed from either of them. I did not receive security from either of my adoptive parents; neither of them cared for me in any way. It was an unfortunate period for me.

Every time I made a simple childhood error, it was another slap in the face or to the body, or screaming and yelling directly in my face, hurting my ears. She spat in my face and threw spoken words to tear me down. She dragged me by the arms through the carpet; she pushed and shoved me around. Violence, lots of constant violence.

With no family to turn to and no one to understand me, I felt hopeless; I did not understand what was happening to me, or why bad things continued to befall me. I was not able to make any mistakes, even if they were accidents. I was not able to learn from them either, even if had been out of my control. I was beat-on and cornered repeatedly for any such things, as if mistakes aren't even an option for me to learn and grow from.

My new family did not like the name Punam (meaning "full moon"). I was renamed Dana. They had two grown sons; one lived nearby, and the other out of town. My new family now consisted of Mom, Dad, two brothers, and a Cocker Spaniel. The elder brother was married with one child, and the younger brother was engaged to be married.

In my transition, I really wanted to wear something familiar, like my frock (a dress that was my normal wear) and flip flops, but I had to wear pants and a sweater instead. I didn't understand why I could not wear what was familiar to me. I had only a few things that I owned, and I wanted those belongings. I had to adapt to wearing clothing that would keep me warm from the cold weather. I also had to learn to live with an animal in the home.

In India, there were many stray dogs, but I was not used to a dog in the home. The Cocker Spaniel was not very friendly. She did not seem to like me at all. I would try to play with her, and she would growl and snap at me. One time, she even bit my forehead. I became fearful and quickly learned not to play with the dog.

I was introduced to new foods (meat, vegetables, and fruits). My new family was made aware of my health deficiencies and provided with a guided nutritional plan for a season. According to my health reports and documentation from BSSK, I had to have certain nutrients to improve my weakened immune system. The food selections were difficult to adapt to because I was not accustomed to the bland food that my family enjoyed.

After a month of adapting to my new family, I began elementary school. I was placed a grade below my natural grade because I did not understand English. They placed me in an English as a Second Language program throughout middle school. I had to learn certain concepts all over again (alphabet and number systems, sight words, picture words, etc.). By middle school, I was able to have basic conversations in English. Most of what I learned in English was through school. I had to grasp the language quickly because

I had no bilingual educational support at home, or familial foundation. My primary socialization occurred at school because there was little communication at home.

In a little town of Iowa, there were mostly Caucasian children, and diversity was rare. Needless to say, I stuck out like a sore thumb. I began to get bullied at school. When I would cut through the field toward home, the boys playing football would set me up, tackle, and pile on top of me. On icy cold days, they would shove me to the ground and shove my face in the snow. They put gum in my hair and taunted and laughed at me. The popular girls plotted against me and picked fights, calling me names in front of my peers.

I could not communicate my thoughts or feelings to my adoptive family because of the language barrier. I didn't learn much from my adoptive family—even basic etiquette. My mom took care of my basic needs to a certain point, considering the language barrier. Looking back, they could have at least modeled the behavior that they expected in the absence of language. My parents were not prepared to raise me as a healthy, socialized non-native in this country. They did not even meet Maslow's hierarchy of needs.

There was a lack of love and emotion expressed. Simple verbal and physical acts of love, like a hug or a kiss, are important to children. My soul and spiritual side were lacking a sense of love and belonging. The lack of communication, bullying at school, and insufficient care were insurmountable. Only now, the bullying and abuse were starting at home as well.

My fear of making any errors or mistakes persisted even as I got older, to the point when, as nature intended, I started my puberty. Growing, going through body changes, I bled in bed. I felt like I was going to be beat for natural issues, and from the first sight of blood, I thought I was dying; I didn't know it was a natural course that all girls go through. With no one to teach me about these changes, how could I have known? I was exhausted, alone, perpetually hungry, and in want of a place to feel safe and cared for.

From day to day, there wasn't any nutritional support. My adoptive mother never intentionally grocery-shopped, and the kitchen cupboards were usually empty. I could not eat regularly, so I lacked energy and focus. My strength was always down, creating health problems and brain fuzziness.

I was always hungry and starving, while my adoptive parents went out to eat, day in and day out. It never crossed their minds that I was also hungry! They couldn't see fit to bring me anything from their frequent trips to restaurants.

Every once in a blue moon, they bought food for two, staying home to eat. My mother always made them a plate, just enough for the two to have and never enough for me. Watching them sit in the living room, eating away while watching TV and sharing food with the dogs, I wondered where my share of food was. Was I that bad to deserve this kind of cruel punishment? Moreover, why were the dogs being treated better than I?

My only means for food were at school. During the summer, it was survival mode. I had to search for food through the kitchen to see if I could find any goodies, anticipating and hoping that I would find something.

Once, I found a box of old graham crackers that I didn't know was old. I climbed up on the counter to grab it to eat, and saw bugs crawling in the box.

My daily mission was to find someone who could feed me. A neighbor, friend, anyone; if not them, it meant a trip to steal candy at a corner store to satisfy my hunger or simply go hungry for weeks.

I always wore clothes that were too big or small, and never received anything new to wear. My wardrobe consisted of the latest from Goodwill.

My adoptive nephews would receive things from the mall, money for college, and their future. As for me, there was little to no financial support.

If I were to ever show up late back home after being outside, I would get locked out. I was invisible, as if I never even existed in front of anyone. I could easily do anything in front of the parents and family and still get ignored.

Holidays were awful. I didn't get to spend much time with any family; the majority of the time it was isolation for me. I didn't have anything to look forward to, including my birthdays.

Getting to school—or anywhere—meant either walking or riding my bike. My parents would even pass me by and refuse to give me a ride. Whether it was cold (winters) with lots of snow, through storms, or heavy rains, I hiked and walked through my sickness, pain, exhaustion, and tiredness.

I couldn't rely on anyone for anything. Rejection was a hard pill to swallow, and people who were my family didn't act like my family.

After going through the trials with my adoptive parents, I came to realize my adoptive mother didn't know her boundaries or limitations, making me suffer from the constant narcissist abuse. I wanted out from the traumatic narcissistic injuries that made me feel like nothing but an abandoned orphan. My adoptive mother certainly made sure to injure my life, both psychologically and emotionally; as a result, I am severely trauma-bound in my psyche.

After going through everything, I had thoughts of suicide due to severe mental depression, where I was not able to get out of bed for weeks and months during the times of oppression.

One mistake from the orphanage caused my life to be in shambles. The orphanage should have taken their time to investigate these people.

Walking with a little bravery in my heart, with my head swung up high, I let myself know I could do this. I sought help from the nearest place I knew... my school! After going through neglect and improper treatment, I finally took my chance, many times, not knowing how to verbalize to the counsellor to let them know about my neglected situation.

After so many nights and months of crying, feeling weary of the life given to me, I needed to be free; I just needed the right opportunity to take me there. The right moment that would open doors for me was there. Then, finally, that moment came when I was eleven years old, taking into consideration what authorities such as a cop had told me: I needed signs and marks on my body to show evidence of abuse, so I could be free. The night prior, all hell broke loose, and finally getting the evidence that I'd been needing gave me the perfect opportunity to show my marks at school.

I came home from my nightly game, which was canceled due to the thick fog. The fog was dangerous to drive in; everybody scattered and hurried on, rushing to go back home—parents, teachers, and children alike. I quickly made my way out the door, hurrying up in my sports gear, shorts, and jersey. With hardly anything on, I got out into the cold and started walking, seeing my breath. Pacing myself fast, I crossed the long school field to get home. Unable to see through the thick clouds, I didn't know I was walking in the wet, muddy ground. I stepped over a broken fence, and I was almost home. Reaching a few more steps, I entered the front door. Feeling the warmth of the house as soon as I came in, I went straight to my room without noticing I was tracking mud. I caught myself at the last minute and walked back to the entrance way to take my shoes off. I anxiously hurried to set things down so I could figure out how to clean this mess I'd created. Tossed back and forth between wanting to get cleaning supplies and having to empty my bladder, I chose to relieve my bladder, and what happened next couldn't be my worst nightmare! The toilet overflowed, water everywhere. Now my attention was divided between the bathroom and the mud on the floor. I didn't know which one to do first! I was torn.

Having two strikes against me, now, I was scared for my life. I could hear my adoptive parents' voices in the basement; I knew they had been hanging mostly downstairs. Crunching for time, I heard footsteps coming up the stairs. Having never been taught to clean, I knew I was in for a new one! I couldn't get to either of the two messes on time before my adoptive mother came up.

My adoptive mother, seeing the mess, instantly went off, yelling, screaming, and cursing. My circumstance became a lit match. I saw demonic possession take over her, screaming, spitting, and cornering me in a small area where I couldn't move. She pushed me, and I almost fell on the dog, who also wanted to take a chunk off my flesh. Though I fought back, tired of the same abuse, she still managed to be stronger than I could bear. She finally got me between the doorpost of my room. I hung on, struggling to keep my strength. I clung onto dear life in between the doorposts, and she finally dug her nails into my skin. Piercing pain went through me. I couldn't hang on any longer, weakening me to let go eventually. She pushed and shoved me until I hit my bedroom floor. She locked me inside as I lay there, crying and feeling so hopeless. I couldn't escape. With nowhere to turn, I kept my wounds fresh for the next day. The following day came with a school day ahead. I anxiously rushed to go out the door and head to school; I couldn't wait for those counsellor doors to open so I could share the evidence. I passed by in the halls several times between my first two classes, here and there. I kept an eye out for the time when someone would be in the office. Communication may not have been my thing when it came to knowing how to express my real emotions and feelings, but I was determined to show on my body what I could not speak in words.

I released myself from my second-period music class, pretending to walk out for a restroom break. I could now see the office light on and open. In desperation, I anxiously slipped into the office so that I could show what had been scaring me for several years. Taking a deep breath, I breathed out a sigh of relief, sitting there and breaking into tears. I uttered a couple of words that I could think of divulging:"I'm scared," and "Please don't take me back." Verbalizing words was not as bad as it seemed; I found (my roar) the power to speak. It was more than I had ever spoken before. Suddenly I didn't feel as mentally dumb. I was finding a little more freedom than before. Nothing was clamping me down or holding me, and I was no longer as fearful to speak my mind. Many times, over again, I felt so much anguish and didn't understand why I couldn't speak! Feeling the freedom of release, I soon spoke out the words, "I'm being abused," and "I'm tired." "Please don't let me go home with them." "I'm scared." "Take me to a shelter." "Anywhere but there!"

Then, *boom*! I was finally feeling relief. I felt the burdens on my shoulders fall off; I don't think I had ever felt that way before!

Experiencing the heaviness fall off me for the first time, the school counsellor wasted no time in talking to the principal regarding my matter—instructions were given to her by the principal to call the Child Protective Services. She walked back in the door and informed me that she must notify CPS. She told me to wait in a private room until their arrival. Two to three hours later, CPS finally arrived to ask me questions.

Why didn't CPS ever arrive sooner in my life? Why didn't any teachers and counsellors take notice that something hadn't been right with me before? With a weight lifting off of me, and knowing that I was finally going to be safe, I was so surprised that it had taken this long. All the burdens that I had been carrying felt like they came crumbling down. I'd never felt this much lighter ever in my life. I was now able to breathe. CPS made me tell my story to them, and as soon as I got done, CPS moved, feeling like they had enough evidence for a case.

With the arrivals of the cops, CPS made me go to my house with them, pulling me out of school, to question the parents that had adopted me. Filing a case, my mother never went to jail. The only slap in her hand was losing her job when the news lady reported the news in the newspapers for the whole town to read. It was the very last time for my mother to become furious towards me. When she got told about my accusations, she rushed towards me angrily and grabbed my arms to insist on seeing the marks that she left on me. I hollered with a loud, shrilling voice, telling CPS to please not let her touch me! I jerked back and swayed closer to the police officer. I didn't want her to touch me; I didn't want to see her face anymore. I was ready to go.

With the assistance of the cop, I got to pack my bags to leave, taking as much I could because I was sure was not ever coming back to see a sight of anything—the dogs, the house, or any of the items in it. It was shelter time; I was on my way to leave. Riding off in the cop car, that was the last time I laid my eyes on this house.

While under the care of the state, the state arranged for the parents to do visitation time to see me, hoping that they could rekindle the parents' relationship with me; it didn't surprise me that both parents refused the state's offer to come see me. This was a way for the state to keep the parents from having their custody rights revoked. I did not understand why the state would go the length to keep relationships together, especially when I had expressed that my life was endangered by terrible abuse and neglect. As both parents were unwilling to cooperate for their custody rights, the state revoked their rights after several attempts to get the parents to cooperate with them. Left with no other option, the state took over completely in my life. Since I had been in the state system, the adoptive parents were willing to give up their legal rights. It didn't make any sense why they went through all the trouble to adopt me.

I wondered if it had anything to do with getting more money for internationally adopting me? As soon as you adopt a child from a foreign country, you usually get more money from the state than in local adoptions. It seemed that could have been a possibility—that I had only been an asset in the adoptive parents' retirement plan, which seems like the most logical thing that makes sense in my mind.

Chapter 5
THE SYSTEM

C hild Protective Services (CPS) removed me from the home of my adoptive family to a safe temporary shelter for youth. I was in the temporary shelter for three to four months and then transferred to a long-term facility to await foster care placement.

I was now eleven and in another center for children who needed protection and did not have a family. Needless to say, after all I had gone through with my adoptive parents, school, bullies, molestation, and forced sexual acts, I was cautious of any system. The one thing I was certain about is that I did not want to relive the trauma I had escaped. I made it my business to express to the officer that I was frightened and did not want to be subjected to further harm and cruelty by others.

My new home was a shelter, but I felt free. The real need for permanent placement in the shelter was revealed. I was free but still struggling emotionally and physically. With all I had gone through, I had no immediate counsel. In retro-spect, I remember the officer recommending family coun-seling during the yo-yo effect between home to shelter and back again. My adoptive parents did not adhere to family counseling as recommended. Instead, they suggested I needed counseling and progressed toward counseling for me. This was important to reduce the communication barriers on my pathway to better mental and physical health.

The shelter provided structure. However, I had only the clothes on my back, official documents, and the belongings I had brought to America from India. The belongings I had accrued from my adoptive parents were given away to Goodwill; they gave everything away. I remained in state custody from age eleven to age seventeen. I now had to begin a new chapter in life.

The state provided a therapist to assist me with socialization and communication so I would not internalize my emotions and retreat into myself. I had to learn how to communicate my feelings effectively and understand my triggers. I underwent intensive therapy for years to address my mental status and develop coping skills of survival in my adaptive environments. Retreating was too easy as I felt safe and out of harm's way, which inevitably caused more harm than good because I would always respond negatively to others.

Long-term care followed my short-term stay. Here, I had more liberty as I settled in with a sense of safety and comfort. I did not have to scavenge or settle for expired food found in deplorable conditions. There had been some pretty desperate moments of starvation when all there was to eat was food with bugs. Now, we were guaranteed three meals a day in long-term care. I was no longer in jeopardy and was grateful that I was better off than some of my peers who suffered with suicidal ideations. In the shelter, the only time we were isolated was when someone tried to harm themselves. Everyone then had to go to their respective places until there was no longer a threat.

The facility was staffed twenty-four hours per day on rotating shifts, which provided a structured daily schedule for feeding, recreation, and outdoor activity. We slept in a shared space in different beds. I was free to socialize with others instead of the isolation I had experienced as an adolescent. All I knew was that the shelter was better than going back to that *living hell* that I'd experienced.

I did not attend public or private school. As a foster child, I attended school at the shelter. School was boring and segregated, and socialization was limited to the shelter. As students, we attended extracurricular events within the community supervised by shelter staff. Schooling at the shelter was credited to our diploma program.

The environment at the long-term care facility was a bit different because of the diverse population. Here, there were many African-Americans. Coming from Iowa's nearly all-white community where I had lived to the diverse population of the shelter was a culture shock. This experience would have a lasting impact on my life.

My new residence shelter had one building that was all girls and another for boys. The population was primarily African-American. I went through a culture shock at first, but the transition ended up being nice. Black people were fun and lively. No matter what life threw at them, they made the best of it. I became very comfortable with the love and happiness they exhibited every day.

SOCIALIZATION IN THE SHELTER

When you leave what you are comfortable with, you realize you have some level of naivety. Because I was used to one form of life in a small circle of Caucasian people without any access to multiculturalism, I had a narrow-minded understanding of the world around me. In this new place though, I did not experience racism and the awful bullying that I had felt in the little country town I came from. My new circle of friends did not look at me differently. Instead, I was accepted among my new African-American community. In Iowa, relationships were based on socio-economic status and similarity. Kids bullied you for the differences in language, status, race, etc.

The advantage I had within my new circle was my experience. I understood everyone because we had similarities. Our situations may not have been identical, but we shared the shelter experience for one reason or another. We were there for problems in our home: Rejection, drugs and alcohol, unsafe home environments, runaway experiences, anger, there were many concerns. Each of us was addressing pain. For me, I was trying to overcome depression from the trauma.

The shift in the atmosphere was amazing. This was the first time I felt secure. I wasn't rejected, mistreated, or bullied like at home. At the shelter, they didn't view me any differently, and my dark, Indian skin tone and accent were accepted and welcomed with open arms. I had not experienced this kind of love in any culture, not even my own.

The African-Americans I've met have been the most important people in my life. They changed my life because they always demonstrated that there was life beyond the racism we experienced with Caucasians. I was intrigued the most by their happiness in the midst of hardship. They didn't always reveal their hard times. They just kept a joy on the inside that I never saw in my family. They knew how to endure life no matter what. Mmm, and their soul food gave me life. Having been accustomed to spicy Indian food, I had finally found some food and friends to enjoy. I also enjoyed getting my hair braided in cornrows. I embraced and was accepted in a culture without bias, and they showed me love I never knew.

This experience was the beginning of my foundation. African-Americans became the vessel to my path to God, family, culture, and love. Black lives really do matter. My friends opened their arms to me and introduced me to a different world. I am who I am because of their love. It is because of their lives that I learned to live a resilient, whole life. God used them to provide a strong foundation as I learned and matured. My childhood had been destined to fail, and I was on the trajectory of a confused and reckless life. My new friends and family became the air I breathed and taught me how to survive and live.

Chapter 6

THE FOSTER HOME

———

By thirteen, I was placed in foster care again, and the cycle continued with interviews of potential foster parents and waiting. Finally, I was matched with new foster parents. New home, new school, new relationships; I hoped this time would be different and I would experience a sense of familial normalcy.

My new foster parent was a real character. She was married and her husband was a supportive system. There were already a few foster children residing in the house. Another child and I were close in age, and the other children were much younger. She also had an adoptive daughter and one biological son. I remember the first day I arrived in Muscatine, Iowa, with my new foster family. There was some resentment from others in the home. However, I had neither the time nor the mood for displaced feelings. I didn't want to waste another second of finding my place in the world.

As time continued, I began to build stronger relationships with the members of the home. Like every other setting, I noticed the youthful indiscretions of others and the

many relevant commonalities that attributed to our placement in foster care (e.g. gangs, drugs, parents on drugs, or
abandonment, to name a few). I was not without my own
share of baggage. We were all at the bottom, and now we
were here in a shared space, making the best of all the challenges that life had presented thus far.

Familial substance abuse that led to foster care placement, growing up in the system, and waiting to be adopted
were our stories. Unstable, life-threatening and addictions
characterized the lives we left behind. There was no rhyme
or reason to why we were here. Our journeys were different
but we were all searching for a sense of belonging.

Nevertheless, I was happy for placement in permanent
foster care. I could finally exhale and face the next phase of
my journey. The constant yo-yo effect of new environments
of the unknown had been exhausting, traumatic, and lacked
stability. These conditions had affected me emotionally,
mentally, and physically. I yearned for a solid foundation
in a stable home with the ability to develop the appropriate
social bonds of family, school, community, and church. I
wanted to live, love, and laugh.

*It was now my freshman year in high school, an exciting
time: new school, new peers, new start. I hoped for a place
that was absent of bullies. I had so many questions about high
school and genuine friendships. My idea of growing up was
exploring new experiences, learning, and understanding the
world around me. I had so many questions. I also had to grow
through these new phases with raging hormones and defiant
behaviors, I had plenty of those. I was ready to get back to*

sports and meet new, like-minded people. Even though I had limitations, I was ready to discover me and the world around me. I was tired of accepting what the world had to offer. If life was going to happen, it would be up to me.

I grew up knowing little about myself, and I was suffering an identity crisis. My life was full of mystery and this puzzle was hard to figure out. The pieces just did not fit. I had so many questions about my origin, and I did not know where to begin the discovery.

My life was a mystery to those who knew me. There were things I did not share with anyone. If someone had asked me, "Who is Dana?" I would be at a loss for words. There is an old adage that says, "To one's self must one first be true." How in the world was I to live a life of purpose holding on to unknown aspects of my current self? Who am I? What is my purpose? I was tired of riding this wave of confusion and aggravation. I felt invisible with a sea of emotions and pain, feeling unimportant, stuck, and living behind a mask. I needed help to find myself. I could not do this alone.

High School in Foster Care

During freshman year of high school, I was ready to get back to sports. I tried volleyball but had to quit shortly after because of a knee injury. The old sprain I had experienced to my knee while with my first family had not been properly treated. The problem resurfaced, only this time, I had to have surgery. My knee would swell to two times the size of my shin, and I could not bear any weight. The lack of treatment caused stress to my strong leg. At sixteen years old, I was faced with two knee surgeries and extensive physical therapy. The surgeons reported a prior ACL tear, old injuries, and new tears in ligaments and the ACL.

In retrospect, my previous care provider left a lot to be desired for adhering to the standards of caring for children. This reality was manifesting more and more. My new family was different. Like everywhere else, some of the children did not like it there. Our parents were disciplinarians. They did not permit bad behaviors like cursing and swearing and other youthful indiscretions we were accustomed to in other places. He expected quiet and respectful mannerisms. We were also required to go to church. To my surprise, he was a pastor.

On Sundays, we were required to be dressed and ready on time to attend church with him. I was expecting other people to show up for church, but we were the only members of the service. While he delivered his sermon, I looked to my foster sisters to see their reaction, and they just went along with everything I could not. It looked like another language to me. I had tried reading the Bible when I was younger, but it was too difficult. I did not waste my time on what I could not comprehend.

At the end of the service, foster dad asked us all to come to the front and line up for prayer. I was expecting him to ask us what we would like to pray about, but he did not ask. Instead, he came to each of us one by one and started praying and prophesying over our lives. When he came to me, he said, "I pray that you will find love." I was shocked and speechless. I looked to one of my foster sisters to ask how he knew this about me. How did he know that I needed and was looking for love?

There was something different about this man. No one had ever spoken into my life in this way. His speaking into my life shattered me. My perspective of him changed; however, I was upset because I needed him to say more. My spirit and soul were thirsty for watering. I thought, "That's it? That's all he has to say to me? He had more to say to my foster sister than me. That's not fair." Eventually, I got over it, and I will never forget him. I believe the minister was a divine intervention sent by God to stand on my behalf. I believe through his obedience to God that a seed was planted in my life as he prayed for my salvation.

It all came together when I gave my life to the Lord in 2005. I received a full revelation that God, through this man, had planted a seed. He discerned something that I did not. As I reflect on that moment, it was my first encounter with God and God used this man to prepare me for what was to come.

Feeling lonely and uncertain, I had a short fuse and low tolerance for some of the nonsense I was experiencing in foster care. The children worked my nerves and sometimes mocked me. I just wanted to be left alone. I remember shoving one girl because she was always taunting me, and it was the only way to get her to leave me alone. My foster parents knew I did not intentionally harm her; unfortunately, it was reported, and the cycle began. I couldn't even protect myself from mean people without being reported. I felt like I was set up with my word against hers. After all, there hadn't been anyone else in the room. I felt like they just did not want me there anymore. The other child corroborated my story, saying, "Whenever foster parents don't want you anymore, they come up with some conspiracy to get rid of you." That is exactly what happened to me.

When would the rollercoaster ride end? Poor health and dental care, I lacked basic needs of shelter, clothing and food. I would maybe get a gift on birthdays and holidays like Christmas. Otherwise, I was on my own for self-care, including haircuts. Foster parents used the state funding received for us children for their families' welfare, vacation, and leisurely living. My peers and I were never allowed to go with our foster families on these excursions. We had no voice about anything that concerned our welfare.

A memorable moment for me was going to a Christian camp in Missouri where I learned to jet ski, water ski, tube, creek stomp, canoe, and more. This was all new to me, and I discovered I had a secret admirer, it was the cutest thing. He sent me roses once while I was in foster care. It was a wow moment, someone cared for me.

When I was sixteen, the DSHS revoked the parental rights of my first adoptive family. I had the choice of foster care until I was eighteen, living on my own as a minor until I was twenty or twenty-one, or being adopted again. I desired to have a family so badly that I chose to try for adoption again. If it did not work, then at least I knew I gave it a try and I would soon be of legal age.

While the foster care system was in search of a new adoptive family, one of my brothers from the first adoptive family made every effort to adopt me but was unable. His mother threatened to denounce his family if he pursued adoption. The fear of losing his family halted the process, and he dropped his application and allowed another family to adopt me.

My options being considered by the state were a couple in New York who had tons of experience with children and a couple in Seattle who did not have any children of their own.

DSHS chose the couple in Seattle as more suitable for my adoption. In the meantime, I was removed from my foster home and placed in another foster home because of the false accusation. Leaving the foster care home was tough because I had developed strong bonds with my foster sisters and did not want to leave. On top of losing my sisters, I was still healing from knee surgery and hobbling on crutches. My body needed time to heal.

I became accustomed to transitioning from place to place. I continued to push through unfamiliar territory and healing in the aftermath of my surgery. In the wake of all the transition, I was preparing to meet the parents from Seattle who had been chosen to adopt me. They spent some time getting acquainted with me. We shopped for new clothing and a prom dress since they knew I was getting ready to attend my first prom soon. I never expected to go shopping, and it was a really good feeling. The meet and greet went well, and they really liked me. The adoptive mother was white, and the father was Indian. They did not have any children of their own. I was their first child and a teenager at that. The adoption was finalized.

Preparations were underway as my new parents remodeled their basement into a living area. My new space had a bedroom, private bath, and a living area for arts and crafts. It was beautiful and generous of them. I had never had anyone care for me in this way. I was surprised and happy, and all the deadlines were met swiftly. Adoptions are much quicker in America than they are overseas. The time had come. I had to say goodbye to all my new friends and high school peers. I prayed and hoped this adoption would be different and that my new family would love and care for me as their own.

FOSTER SISTERS AND I

Dana

Dana is a beautiful 16-year-old girl who would one day love the opportunity to model professionally. She is a very likeable girl with high ambitions for her future. One of these hopes is to grow up in a family that will accept her and love her for who she is. We can help to make her dreams come true!

Chapter 7

THE BONDAGE OF THE SECRET LIFE OF AN ADOPTED TEEN

One chapter closed and a new one began in Washington State. In January 2000, I flew to Seattle. I was seventeen and my adoption was official. Not only was I experiencing a new environment, but a new state. It was the beginning of my sophomore year in high school and I had to get used to a new school, new people, and my new home. This was a new experience for my adoptive family too. They had no previous experience with adoptive or biological children. I was their first child as well as their first teenager.

I was nervous and feeling uncertain. Once again, I began feeling awkward, wondering what comes next. How do I develop social bonds with these people? I had so many questions: How do I fit in? How do I know what's right and wrong since there had been no clear distinction or guidance given to me most of my life?

The lack of appropriate socializations left me clueless of appropriate expectations besides those that just didn't feel right. My new mom had a therapy degree and a private, in-home practice. Maybe she would provide counseling for me. Perhaps with her expertise, she could help me remove the barriers to feeling whole (feelings of awkwardness and trapped emotions). Do my feelings and experiences have a name? I need help. I was confused about everything.

There was a bit of a culture shock as there were many differences in my new family and home. My former family was of European descent and my new family was of mixed cultures, both European and Indian. They let me change my name from "Dana Mary Schneider" to Dana Priyanka Sen. My middle name Priyanka was prophetic, meaning, "is loved," and Sen reflects my new family name. I never understood the meaning of love. I desired love. I discerned that I was only pitied by others, and pity does not mean love. I equated to some superficial love that was temporary.

I have high hopes for love and new beginnings. I quickly learned that there was something missing. This seemingly normal family struggled with some kind of imbalance.

My mother was a great cook and I enjoyed her food. She had many talents and gifts. She loved quilting and her work was impeccable. She also enjoyed scrapbooking. She had so many wonderful items to get her creative juices flowing. She was talented in so many ways. However, she struggled as a professional therapist. She was good at helping others work through their problems, but she struggled at taking her own advice at home. It was clear that she was having difficulty psychoanalyzing me. She didn't understand me and did not understand my behaviors. Our relationship was short-lived.

My adoptive dad was along for the ride to appease my adoptive mom. He was an intelligent man: knowledgeable about stocks and software industries and whatever high tech he was doing in his company. Following the stock market and reading books and magazines were his favorite things to do. He enjoyed studying and educating himself about the world. His morning routine consisted of an early breakfast of half cooked oatmeal with lots of milk. Off to the Seattle transit he went every day for a hard day's work. He was a hard worker with impeccable work ethics and known as a loyal friend and colleague.

There seemed to be a natural father daughter bond, or at least so I thought. We enjoyed outings together and he showed me the world through his lens. He was friendly, sociable, and adaptable to the adoption process. His natural ability to connect was important to me. I yearned to learn, grow, and become a productive citizen.

I felt a natural father daughter bond for a while, so I thought, because he took me out to places to show me around, made me feel welcomed and introduced me to a few of his coworkers to make me part of his life. It seemed he did more so then his wife did. He seemed more social then she was and he seemed he could have gotten the grasp of it a little more than she did. Life seemed like it was flowing here and there from the beginning and I was starting to settle in. I didn't think much of it but I was yearning to learn how to grow up and get a job and learn how to live on my own. Everything every teenager wants to know in being prepared for the world and moving out on my own but yet it seemed they didn't know that part of me and or even have the slightest clue as to what someone my age needed or wanted. How could they? They were so unprepared.

Even though I was a teenager, I noticed that they were starting to treat me like a little child and not my appropriate age. Yes, they were forewarned by my social worker from back in Iowa that I was dealing with some circumstances yet they were so unprepared for that at the same time, unprepared in how to raise a teen and the age of a teen and a troubled teen. All teens want is to be prepared for the world, have self-confidence, and discover themselves and know what they want to do. I felt so behind with my teen life, I wasn't taught anything, nothing was talked through with me as I was growing up, it just felt like whatever life gave me, I had to accept and now that I had a little more freedom, I felt so behind in everything and wasn't ready for the big world.

I happened to finish the rest of my physical therapy in Washington and learned how to walk again, strengthening my legs all over again but had to get my leg manipulated and back in surgery to get scar tissue broken down since I couldn't bend my leg appropriately. I was working through that while I happened to meet more of my new family members from India and Virginia and their friends as time passed.

Now living in Seattle, starting a new year, trying again to establish some type of grounding, to get stability in a teenager's life, meeting new friends at school, new routines and rules being set at home, finding out where places are and how everything is going to work. Getting familiar with the area, I rode the transit first so I could get around. I did have my adoptive dad to thank for that, he showed me how to ride the transit and showed me what to do when it came to transit survival skills but I needed more than that since I had been needing survival skills for many other things but did not learn since neither of them taught me anything else. I just had to go to school, do my studies and get help for my education and tutoring so I could keep up with my class and finish all my basic classes for high school; that was the goal at least.

By the time December rolled around, I was given a vacation opportunity to go back to India with my new family. This was my second winter with my new adoptive family. For our first holiday together, we stayed in Washington. They planned for us to be in New Delhi and Calcutta, India for the holidays this year, Christmas and New Years, and then return home; we stayed for a month or more.

I had an opportunity to see my native country and experience the culture without going back to Pune, India, my last home when I first left India. When we arrived in Northern India, I was hoping at one point to go to the southwest part of India, to revisit my hometown, where I could see the orphanage and possibly see somebody that I grew up with. We never got there and stayed mainly up north and east. The first part of the stay was exciting because I was going to meet my new grandparents and other relatives of the family like my dad's sister, etc. Witnessing some of their traditions of their ways; they initially accepted me as their granddaughter and part of the family. I experienced some of the shopping, a spa in the area, along with a traditional family wedding because my dad's sister was getting married and we had to be part of the small family wedding party. I also got to have some of the foods around the area, with a long train ride to see the countryside. As the stay went on, tension began to grow and I was starting to be ignored by the adoptive family and their behaviors started shifting, I specifically noticed this with my mom. I noticed she started smoking with my dad, this habit she picked up in India couldn't be stopped later on back home which was a problem but India caused a major shift and change in their behaviors and mood changes. I started feeling the tension and more of the awkwardness. Our last day in India, New Year's Day 2002, we left to go to Singapore. Singapore was our last stop for a day before heading home. Singapore was very clean and pretty and I felt like it put Washington to shame, that's how squeaky clean and pretty it was.

After visiting Singapore, we were on our way back to Seattle. Arriving back home, the tension and atmosphere became thick, lots of feuding and drama started to grow quickly, constantly being verbally attacked with different allegations of being rebellious, uncontrollable and breaking them down mentally and physically with their life. It got to the point of them calling the police on me twice. One evening, without warning and without any options, they told me to pack and get ready to leave. Little did I know my relationship with my adoptive parents was coming to an end. I did things and they did things that escalated to this point which seemed like a point of no return. I didn't realize I was going to face my biggest fear, which was rejection and abandonment again. They forced me into their friend's truck to take me away, I did not want to go. I was struggling to get away because I had no idea who this person was or where they were taking me. They held me by the hand and thigh with a seat belt to restrain me. As they turned onto the freeway, I opened the door and tried to escape. The stranger took me to the emergency room and told the doctors that I was suicidal, and I was involuntarily committed, they took their word. My parents threw me away, they didn't want me around anymore. No one would listen as I cried for help.

I was placed in the University of Washington mental ward for evaluation for a few days. I was outraged. I had been with my new family for thirteen months. They abandoned me to a mental ward with all of my hopes and dreams as a teenager for stability and comfort. I was placed in a Bellevue Washington shelter for two weeks, was moved to Vashon Island Washington Shelter and placed temporarily in an all-girls group home for transition to independent living at age eighteen, all in one year. *What a ride!*

Was it over? *NO!* I got moved into the independent program. I never saw the second adoptive family ever again. They never came and visited me, they never called me personally to ask me how I was doing, and they never invited me to any holidays or came to celebrate any of my big events, wheather it was a birthday or graduation. They gave me false hope and lied that they would never give me up or reject me like my first adoptive parents.

When I first got saved in 2005, I was told by the Lord that I was going to run into some people from my past and little did I know it would be my second adoptive family. This was God's way of teaching me about the power of forgiveness.

Through lessons of forgiveness I was able to receive my healing to forgive and move on from people who caused me harm. I apologized for anything wrong I may have done. I forgave them. They never apologized to me. When I first found out that I had to face and forgive people from my past, I had no desire to forgive. I downright refused to forgive people who caused me harm. How do you forgive people who meant you no good? It was a hard pill to swallow. I had to face every dark place in my life.

I had some deep wounds from my second family and it was hard to get over them. The most hurtful of them all was rejection, they promised never to reject me, it was a *lie*. I was placed in a group home that cared more about me than they did, they never even came to visit me, call me or bother to send a Christmas card or birthday card. They told me that they were going to be my family forever. None of it made sense. Why would they hurt me?

I forgave them. I needed a family more than anything and I thought that they were going to be there for me. They were no different than the rest. I thought this time would be different because she had counseling experience, this would be a good fit for me, a place where I could receive the counseling, nurturing, and teaching that I needed. Instead they pushed me away and kicked me to the curb, adding unnecessary baggage to my life. She did not care about me; her love was fake. I expressed that I enjoyed being around her husband because he was a real father figure and there was nothing to be alarmed about. It seemed neither of my families was equipped to handle the challenges of raising a teenage girl who needed guidance.

After all that I had been through, emotional stability, personal skills and a pathway to maturity were essential to my growth and development as a teenager. Counseling was necessary, but not ethical in this relationship. I needed counseling outside of the home. This relationship was strained and did more harm than good. There needs to be caution in the placement of children with people that understand their challenges. I needed a constructive hand in helping to achieve and have a stable life than to be fed to the wolves. Adoption should be granted to families that have that physical and mental capacity to raise adopted children.

Time after time, I was faced with consequences based on the reality of others versus the facts of my lived experience. I was not given a chance. I was hurled into an involuntary commitment because of my parent's inability to provide a non-threatening environment where I could thrive without the recurring thoughts of my lived past. I had no idea what they were even talking about.

They assumed by some notion they brought me to the Lord through church involvement…false! It is not a man who can draw another man to the Lord, it takes the spirit of the Lord to draw a man and that man has to show the true love of God. That is where I believe they failed. I do not believe they demonstrated the real love of God. I was tired of them victimizing me as if I were the cause. They were hiding behind their own agenda. Who were they to judge what they didn't know for themselves, after all, they just dropped me off there. I was never trained. The word says, "train up a child…." I saw their pretentious religion but not practical application in their daily lives. They did not lead by example or show me how to love. They were sheep in wolves clothing. One moment they loved me, and then another moment, they seemed to hate me. Was this out of pity? I would see them smoking and drinking. Were they a Christian family? They would not have done that because of God's law.

Looking back, it seems everything was about them with little regard for my emotional well being. Their emotional walls were hindering a true relationship. I could not wrap my mind around any of this, all of it was a breakdown in communication. There were two sides to this disaster. I was a perceived threat. I was a lost soul looking for love and a need to belong before I met them.

My life was complicated by the deep scars of abuse and rejection. I wanted and needed help. Learning that my new parent was a counselor was promising. I would finally get help. I hoped to learn how to be a better communicator. I longed for the quality of the relationships she developed with others through counseling.

We never saw eye to eye; she only valued her side of the story. Thus, there was nothing to be gained from continuing to try at a relationship. She told me to never write again. All I wanted was to come to forgiveness, again, they dismissed me. You cannot measure a person by their past. The only person who could tell my truth, is me. It was my lived experience. They would talk down to me as if I was stupid, like I didn't know what I was talking about and I had no say on any matter, I had no opinions as if I hadn't a mind of my own.

You cannot fix someone when you need to be fixed yourself. Jesus had to appear unto me to let me know that He was real and that He was the one who changed my life. He made me a new creature with a new identity. For that, I am grateful and honored to be the King's kid, because I thank God every day that His ways are higher than our ways and His thoughts are higher than our thoughts. He does not judge me from the outside but looks at my heart.

If it had not been for the Lord on my side, I don't know where I would be. He knew and did not give up on me. He knew everything; my lacking of love and affection from being abandoned.

PERCEPTIONS VS. LIES OR THE TRUTH OF WHO I REALLY WAS

Be careful about what you think of others and what you say about them for the same He will do unto you. Do not be quick to judge for things are not always what they seem. It was difficult to respond favorably to the lack thereof. I was not wanted in their life and they made that clear. I learned to appreciate the protection I felt by the group home staff, they showed me love.

They were like a shield of protection from others. They taught me to take responsibility for my actions and to know that all things were not my fault. I no longer hold grudges against others because Jesus forgave me of my past and I must forgive others. I was removed from the home of an abuser. I needed to learn how to manage my mental health to develop healthy relationship beyond the physical and mental trauma I experienced. It has taken time for me to be delivered from an unhealthy state of mind to deal with other human beings effectively. I am a miracle, a sinner saved by grace. It has taken a lot of time and patience to love again. I have fought and continue to fight my own demons and insecurities from what lies deep within. I had to fight the pain of abuse, rejection, and neglect.

I am a new creation in Christ and behold old things have passed away and all things have become new. He made me whole and I now know that I am a child of the living God. He knows the thoughts that He has towards me. Thoughts to prosper me and bring me to an expected end. I was lost but now I am found and I was blind but now I see. I will never be the same in Jesus's name. It doesn't matter what other people think or say about me as long as I know who I am in Christ, I can stand on that and know that I am the King's kid and I know that I am going to be with Him in paradise.

Inclusion, my second adoptive parents were just not ready to adopt a teen, with no experience of a child from birth to teen but as well as they were not equipped with knowing how to handle a teen with trauma even though they were forewarned that I could have had detachment issues, etc. I was a teen who dealt with PTSD and trauma that had not been resolved, and I believe the family bit off more than they could handle. I think they could have handled a little more responsibility if they were more equipped in how to handle and take care of someone with such great needs; I don't think they were and this was the reason why my second adoption failed as well.

The easiest thing they could do was to get rid of me. That experience certainly brought abandonment and rejection feelings all over again in my life, hovering over me like a dark cloud. It was the hardest pill to swallow and the most painful memories to have along with other things in the past. I cannot be mad at them for trying even though they did not count up the cost for what it is. I love and appreciate the hard journey that I endured because I would not be who I am now if it wasn't for it and I would not be able to be in another state if it wasn't for the situation that got me here so that way I can finally be stable in my life.

Chapter 8

REFLECTIONS

———

In reflection, I went through two failed adoptions because of the system and its failure to properly diagnose me and match my needs i.e. personality, personal needs, and mental wellness; getting tossed home to home and not giving me the proper protection and support when it came to the adoptions, shelters, and foster home systems.

In my first chapter, I titled it "Abandonment," thinking and feeling that I was abandoned and that my birth family didn't want me but in reality, when I got older, I discovered that I was child trafficked and those abandonment feelings were not correct. The abandonment really did not come to play a role in my life until I first came to America from India through my first adoption which continued from there into my latter years. Most of us adoptees usually feel rejected and abandoned. I came to realize that is a way too familiar territory for many of us and that it is the biggest lie that completely overtakes us with true feelings of abandonment and rejection. Those feelings mislead us, and those unknown answers lie to us to make us feel and think that our birth families do not really want us.

In reality, that is not the case for every adoptee. Some get kidnapped from the hands of their birth parents and others have different experiences. It is our job to really find out the truth because not everyone's stories are the same. My book title, *Abandoned but Not Forgotten*, was derived from my constant feeling of abandonment from the time that my kidnapping took place in India to walking through a life of no one wanting me in America.

There is a simple nursery rhyme that explains this foster and adoption system and the whole child welfare in general called *Hansel and Gretel*. *Hansel and Gretel* is the story of two kids whose father married another woman. That woman doesn't like kids for whatever reason, the woman gives a suggestion to the children's father to get rid of the kids by abandoning them in the forest since they were struggling economically. This would allow them to save money, so they would not have to worry about the kids. Getting rid of the kids was pretty much a survival tactic.

The kids get abandoned in the forest with neither their father or the stepmother returning for them the first and second time over again. The second time, children could not return after the breadcrumb trail was eaten up by the birds after Hansel placed them there to help guide them back to their own house and return to their father. Instead, the kids found themselves lost in the wilderness and somehow find themselves at the candy house after wandering around. A witch sees them, enticing them by feeding them and locks them in the house, making Gretel cook and clean for her like a slave and fatten Hansel so she can eat Hansel as well as Gretel.

This is a resemblance to the broken system of the child welfare system, whether it is by orphanage, the adoption system, the foster home system, shelters, or group homes. Let me give you an example of how the children's welfare system is compared to the Hansel and Gretel story. The dysfunctional part of the family, whether it is to drugs, alcohol, financial issues, or abuse, leads to the separation of a healthy lifestyle a child could gain. This thus creates a vacuum for the system to step in, as well as creates an outlet for the family to discard the children or the children to be taken away.

The forest represents the lost journey, total confusion, and lost identity the children have when it comes to their own life. The trail of breadcrumbs that gets eaten up by the birds are the vanishing children who never return home, which leads the children to becoming a lost cause.

The candy house is like the system, it looks good on the outside. But the inside is really ugly. This is designed to attract the children but, in the end, it becomes a prison.

Some people in the system often have alternative motives, and the gold in the candy house represents the wealth of funding available in the system where these people will take advantage of the opportunity to manipulate the system for their own benefits.

Those people in the system are like the witch in the candy house who will take advantage of the cause and foundation of the system, allowing them to prey and take advantage of the children's vulnerabilities for personal gains. That's when the structure of the service becomes deceptive because of the neglect of the children. The cage in the candy house represents the sentiment of the children which causes them to feel imprisoned like many other children, in wherever they are thrown. This is not a lifestyle of freedom but of bondage because once the children get out of the system, they are frequently left open and vulnerable, unprepared for anything to take place in their own lives. The lack of confidence for the big world manifests in each and every insecure child.

Wherever the state has their hands on, there seems to be something missing that is hidden from the public eye. A reformed change needs to take place when it comes to the system of welfare for children. Children's lives have been endangered, from infants to young adults and a lot has been at stake because of the children's vulnerability and the position they have been left in. They are vulnerable and naive from not being taught in a healthy upbringing as well as not covered in education or receiving proper health and mental treatment from trauma that they have possessed, alongside being tossed from home to home. Children's lives are at stake since they are just thrown out there in the world without properly being equipped for life's encounters. Boundary lines are blurred and their model of what a healthy relationship looks like is broken.

Being bounced around from home to home did not just leave me vulnerable but it left me open for anything to happen to me, whether it's being trafficked again or whether it's someone preying on me. I'm left open for anything that can lead to damaging my life. Proper training and boundaries are needed, especially for the upbringing of a child that grows up to being a young adult, due to the fact that the majority of the kids that are left hanging in the child welfare system are susceptible for anything to take place in their lives.

In the aftermath of foster care and adoption, hindsight is 20/20. The system leaves a lot to be desired and new guidelines should be considered. There needs to be an intensive interview process to assure that the welfare and safety of children is secured. If more consideration was given to barriers associated with culture, language, age divisions, and most of all, the trauma associated with my life in general, perhaps the system could have reduced the harm to me and other children with appropriate placement.

ABOUT THE AUTHOR

Dana Priyanka Hammond is a mental health paraprofessional and bestselling author of Amazon's hot new release, *Tear the Veil (Volume 2)*, co-authored with eighteen fearless visionary leaders and speakers. In addition, she shares the love of her culture in her book *Delicious Vegetarian Dishes: The Top 10 Recipes with Unique Flavor of Indian Cuisine*, both in print and eBook on Amazon, Barnes & Noble, Apple, and more.

Dana is a light of hope to many as she shares her story of abduction from her family by human traffickers. Through grace, she was rescued by police and transferred to an orphanage and later adopted by an American family. Dana lived a life of abuse and neglect as she moved through the system from adoption, foster care, and shelters, while suffering from PTSD and narcissistic abuse.

Through her Indian cuisine cooking show on Facebook, Instagram, and Twitter, she connects the world to her culture and advocates against child sex trafficking, neglect and abuse within the adoption and foster care systems, and world hunger. Today, she joins the ranks of eighteen fearless visionary leaders to speak out against atrocities known to mankind.

She is a new mom to Samar Evelyn Cadence Hammond. Advocacy is more important than ever before to break the cycle of child abuse toward pathways of healing, restoration, and the fullness of life.

Website: danapriyankahammond.com
http://www.humantraffickinginc.com
Facebook: dana.priyanka.32
Twitter: @dana_priyanka
YouTube: Dana Priyanka Hammond
Instagram: danapriyankahammond

SUMMARY

This book is about the life of an abandoned girl who manages to transform her life from abandonment, rejection, and abuse to glory, deliverance, and life. It is a reflection of her life from abandonment to deliverance with God. This book will also show her therapeutic growth in life, showing people that if she could do it, they can also.

A story of encouragement and inspiration about the journey of a little girl, abandoned at a train station in Pune, India. Discover how she rose above it all to proclaim her liberty.